Impolite Thoughts

Esther Sherman

PublishAmerica

Baltimore

ISBN: 1-60441-895-8
PUBLISHED BY PUBLISHAMERICA, LLLP
www.publishamerica.com
Baltimore

Printed in the United States of America

Dedication

*For Patrick…in every day, everything that we do,
you are loved and remembered.*

Acknowledgments

In looking into the work that has gone into this book, the emotional and physical work, I have become wholly aware that I do not have myself alone to thank. However, the list of people who have inspired me is much too long to be given in a name by name manner. To my family, my mother in particular, thank you for your continued support and encouragement. It has been your guidance that has made me the woman that I am. To those who have been family without sharing any genetic resemblance, I love you and your support is valued. To my professors and Wanda, thank you for teaching me about life in spite of my sarcasm and attendance record. To the friendships formed within the boundaries of CBU, thank you for acceptance, compassion, humor, and endless moments of inspiration. To the friends of my youth who have remained, thank you for memories that will never change and love that has given me strength when I held none of my own. To those who know me, I mean sincerely know me, thank you for seeing something that I never quite understood without you. Now, for that which is most important, thank you to my G-d. My life, my breath, and my being are by your mercy alone. I know that I fail, but when I succeed, these are the people that deserve the thanks.

Impolite
Thoughts

Chapter One
The Things My Pride Won't Tell You

We often spend our lives pretending to be who we think others believe us to be. From putting on make-up in the morning, to discussing topics that bore us to tears, we try to be that person. We try to fit the mold that we assume we were designed to fit. I don't fit that mold. In my life, there have been few people with whom I have been able to be sincere. The rest, the rest have seen what I have wanted them to see. This is the truth. On these pages, in this work, there is truth.

The Ghosts of Darkness

A broken host of memories
Play silent through the night
Crashing in and drifting back
Retreating from the light

Something displaced in the past
I now can see so clear
I shadow my face with honest lies
Hoping no one can hear

The looming ghosts I've left behind
They whisper all that's been
The memories I once forgot
Now lurk beneath my skin

Running from the darkness
But night I know will come
The voices continue echoing
Until the rising sun

There is no way to escape them
They have brought me to fall here
And at the midnight hour
Their unspoken scenes are near
Wrapped in pure confusion

Resting in unadulterated pain
Surrounded by my past alone
And the bitter chill of rain
Closing my eyes as dawn breaks

Across another sleepless night
Scattering my vicious thoughts
With the coming of the light

I drag myself from tired space
And move about the day
Waiting for my quiet ghosts
And the memories they play

Pain

Being sappy and pathetic is worthless to me now. My broken heart still finds a way to beat somehow. How could I have been this blind, the same way as before? Why do I insist upon breaking through an open door? The easy way I leave alone…That's it though, right? I leave alone. I always have and I always will. I don't deserved to be loved…I especially do not deserve a love that can touch me; a love who lays next to me…in whose arms I awake. I don't deserve that. I never have and I never will.

That's why. Why do I keep trying? I swore I wouldn't do this again…proving myself a liar. I swore I wouldn't fall…I wouldn't let him in. How many times I swore it? G-d Himself can barely count! Still, I am a liar. I let him past my smile. I let him past my eyes. I let him past every inch of flesh and now I bear the scars.

I said I would not love again. Oh, how I uttered lies. I promised not to let someone, not to feel this pain. "Tis better to have loved and lost…" I haven't lost and yet alone! To cry is shame and brings forth pity from every eye that falls.

Pity is for weakness; a mark that you have failed. I will not stand for it. I must keep moving. As long as I am moving I do not have to see me. Don't you see? It is me that I despise. It is my voice I cannot stand to hear and my face I wish not to see.

My life is a lie; it is a smile that shadows the depths of my own disgust. I mock humanity because it is human. I mock men because I cannot be strong. I mock women because I cannot be weak. I mock myself in silence, so that no one hears my words.

Love knows my face and my smiles; but it does not know my secrets. It cannot see my lies. Love knows only happiness and sees only what is good. It falls for my façade and awakes with my disgust. I swore never again. Never again would a man's touch scar me; but your scars were that of tenderness.

Your touch was that of love. How was I to know those scars would be much greater? Don't you see my turmoil? Are you bold enough to see my lies? It is not modesty, nor humility. I do not seek your compliments or wait upon your affection. It is not for me that I cry out. It is out of an utter disgust of who I am, who I have been, and how many have suffered because I first drew breath.

That is my secret. That is what I hide when my voice goes cold. That is the fire that lashes from my tongue at whatever object it can strike. That is why I push. That is why I hide. That is why I wear a mask and why I shield my eyes. There is the truth…the reality of my anger; the answer to my pain. I have traveled the world to escape me and beside me I remain. Now you know the truth. Do with it what you will.

The Kiss

The town, the building, the place
I remember when
The smile, the touch, the embrace
Just as if now was then
The day, the hour, the minute
I remember when
The second, the moment, the kiss
Just as if now was then

Forgotten

Here you were
But now you're not
You knew me once
But then forgot

Or did you ever
Even know?
Was it my pain
That made you go?

The pain you've seen
Pour from my eyes
When all you gave
To hold were lies

Tears keep falling
Upon my skin
Life grows cold
And dark within

You're the nightmare
That never ends
You're the worst
Of all my sins

Emptiness echoes
Through me now
I must get back
To then somehow

Before you left
And broke my heart
Before your silence
Ripped me apart

When here you were
But now you're not
You loved me once
But then forgot

Forgetfulness

Forgetfulness, I envy
To no longer know the cost
To not remember the moments
The love which I have lost
For to not remember you
May be an easy task
Compared to moving on
Is that too much to ask?

The Little Black Dress

It is neatly folded on the end of the bed. I don't know why I bothered to fold it; it needs to be washed anyway. It is just force of habit I suppose. It is slightly fancier than I would like, but it fits me well. It sits just above my knee and gently hugs my curves. It has frills on the sleeves; I could do without that.

It is a little black dress. This morning it hung in the closet. I picked it up and looked at it for a little too long. It's not my "little black dress", it just happens to be one. It is my funeral dress.

I wore it last December for my uncle Casey. Black: it represents sadness and pain. A bath is running in the background and my feet are aching. This morning I slipped into neat black heels. I looked nice, really I did. Ironic I suppose. Normally it would be Shiva, no clean clothes, certainly no heels. It's not. She wouldn't have wanted that. I sat in the pew.

I cried. Something I haven't done in a while. It is weird the things you remember; sitting there looking at an entire life. I worked with her and we were pretty close. Honestly, she was close with everyone. She was that type of person. It wasn't unexpected but I don't know if that makes it any easier. They sang "Heaven is a wonderful place". They played that at my brother's funeral. That got to me. I miss him.

It's been three years and I miss him.

I didn't wear black to his funeral. I proudly wore yellow and purple, Lakers' colors. He would have hated to watch them lose three days later. It's odd the things we remember.

I cried. I leaned on a friend I love dearly and he reminds me of a friend that isn't there. It's odd the things we remember.

I closed my eyes for a second and I was in the passenger seat of a van a long way from here. I was happily talking. I can almost hear the laughter in my voice and the amusement in his. That was back when I was always learning, always listening. It's odd the things we remember.

The bath is ready. I unfold the dress and give it one last look before throwing it in a pile with the rest of the laundry. Black: sadness, pain, death.

Petal

I stand and watch a petal fall
As if I am falling too
The sun is looming over me
The sky a denim blue

The ground has caught the petal
But I am falling still
Consumed in clouds of fear
Caught against my will

Tears

The tears I have withheld
And the tears I have beheld
Have fallen side by side
My stubbornness aside

The Sun Went Down

He is not in bed beside me
Thus I am awake still
I know he means no harm
It's just his stubborn will

But the separation of our hearts
Grows with every moment
The love that once exploded
To someone else has went

So I sit here, alone and quiet
Wondering when he'll come
Hoping to rest beside him
Before the rising of the sun

Desperation

Desperation follows me
I cannot escape its grip
My sarcasm serves as solace
But I have not one more quip

Despair

Despair leads us to interesting ends. We make poor decisions, to say the least. When we find ourselves in moments of absolute desperation, there is nothing we would not do. A moral standard keeps some of us from crossing an invisible line. Some of us have no such standard. The distance between one who is desperate and one who is not is the extent to which they would go to sustain their view of life.

Separation

Considering the pain I'm in
I'd say I'm doing rather well
Other than fire and brimstone
This is nothing at all like hell

Away

Agony has filled my veins
It permeates every thought
My own decisions, foolishness
G-d, what have I wrought?
I can feel my every heartbeat
And every one, it aches
I am waiting for the moment
When all reason finally breaks
I have walked a million miles
Just trying to escape
But nothing can release me
From underneath this cape
I am burdened and I alone
For this has been my doing
I listened to the lies I heard
The whispers and the wooing
I left all the home I knew
Now I am left waiting
I am left alone in silence
Myself, I am left hating
My choice, my choice, my failing
And now there is only dark
For this foolishness and pain
This shall be my mark
I am barely breathing
My chest I scarcely raise
For without The One I knew
Upon an empty life I gaze

Confusion

Everything is rhyming
Everyone is dense
It's all in perfect timing
It just doesn't make sense
I see the truth I'm finding
I know not what I mean
In darkness I am crying
In light I am unseen

Lying

Brokenness is shining
Behind these eyes that smile
Denying constant pain
And the torment of this style
As tears threaten appearance
Laughter floods this place
I cannot refrain from humor
Or you may just see my face
The scars left by my failings
Rest just beneath the skin
Covered by the lies I've told
To keep you from my sin
The fabric of my very flesh
Has kept you from what's real
The silence of my very lips
Hardens this heart that's still
Our eyes will catch one moment
And you'll wonder in the glance
If perhaps that was the truth
Perhaps your only chance
But then these eyes will smile
Hiding every ounce of pain
And again I'll disappear
Amidst the pounding of the rain

Darkness' Cape

The night crept in as a silent thief
Moonlight bending to find relief
It draped itself across the room
Then stood in silent, waiting gloom
Its presence drew me through the door
To behold an answer asked of Yore
But I fell prey to its dreadful cold
The question alone I'm left to hold
No manner of creature can yet escape
The silence that lingers 'neath darkness' cape

I Lied

I lied to you,
so many times I lied
I never spoke the truth,
I never even tried
I was afraid to speak,
afraid that you could see
If I spoke those words aloud,
I just may cease to be

Patrick

I will never forget the look on my mother's face when she woke me. There were so many tears. She couldn't even explain. I could not understand her trembling words. She said one word audibly and it seemed as if my world had shattered. "Patrick" she said. There was nothing else to say. There was nothing else that could have brought this pain into her eyes. I remember sitting back down on the bed and waiting. Waiting for the sky to fall, waiting for hell to freeze. I was waiting for anything that made more sense than him not coming home.

Awaking Loss

A crisp December morning
Awakes covered in frost
The light refracting gently
Off a moment counted lost

Begging

Remembering the moment
My knees fell to the ground
Pleading for his voice
For just one more sound
Begging for one moment
Just one more day with him
Inside of my aching soul
Tears cause me to swim
Just one more time to see him
And know that he is near
Just one more time to smile
And hold his laughter dear

Silence

The silence still is ringing
Out above the singing
The cheerful melody
Has lost its tune on me

Cursing

I've never been good at cursing
I've never really tried
I never had a reason
Until you left my side

Reflecting Truth

Behind a mask I'm hiding
So you won't know my name
Blending in with broken glass
Inside a beaten frame

As you walk past I see you
But am offered not one glance
The dreams bursting within me
Will die without a chance

Invisible to the outside world
Remains a heart in need
Behind the smiles and laughter
There is a tear-filled plead

Upon a wall I'm hanging
Waiting for you to see
That the one you're walking past
Is much more you than me

I reflect only what I'm given
I'm weary of holding lies
I pray you'll stand before me
Without that nice disguise

To be real for just one moment
I hope you will embrace
Let yourself feel the truth of pain
That a tear may bless my face

I'm holding you as you walk past
I see every scar from here
But still you keep on walking
And still I don't know where

From behind a mask emerging
So you will know my name
Picking up the broken glass
Hoping you will do the same

Faking

Faking life is tiring
You never can let go
If you stop for just a moment
Then everyone will know

Falsehoods

Sometimes overwhelming,
always worth the lie
I hide for my existence;
it's either that or cry

Emptiness

An empty page in an empty book,
An empty face cast an empty look

Next to the bed there lay a journal; a place of hiding for a haunted soul. As calloused fingers embraced its leather binding, it revealed pages as empty as the heart that held it. His eyes dripped upon the lines, but not one word was uttered.

An empty shadow on an empty wall,
An empty soul takes an empty fall

The night was growing denser and a lamp in the living room provided the only light. His form was cast upon the wall as his shadow lifted a bottle, with every sip the night grew darker.

An empty moment in an empty day,
An empty religion kneels to pray

With the morning light he lifts himself off the cold floor. He wanders into a dusty building through large oak doors. The minister speaks and no one hears. The entire congregation carefully positions themselves to pray. In a crowd of people on their knees, he stands and cries out to God.

An empty touch on an empty face,
An empty faith offers empty grace

A young man shakes his hand hesitantly as he leaves. His tattered clothes and bloodshot eyes are all the man can see. The unshaved face bears the touch of pain that has made himself ignored.

An empty house in an empty town,
An empty woman wears an empty gown

He gazes up at her window; the window where he stood the night he proposed. Eight years ago, she committed to him there. In the light she stands wearing a dress of white. Tomorrow she will commit herself to another. The bottle grows warmer in his hand and his heart grows colder with its touch. She chose a life he could not give her and he chose to forget life without her.

An empty laugh in an empty place,
An empty eye looks at empty space

As he gazes upon all that his home is to him, a derisive laugh escapes his lips. There is nothing worthy of laughter.

An empty tear on an empty cheek,
An empty day makes an empty week

The bed remains half-empty and his heart remains half there. As he lays there in discomfort his eyes drift to the empty space beside him; the void of all that was. There are no words, only the shimmering quiet of absent life written upon his cheek.

An empty love in an empty heart,
An empty smile becomes an empty art

So easily he fools them, with laughter and with joy. He covers his
pain with a façade and all are convinced of truth. A ring still wraps
his finger, though another man's wraps hers. He smiles through a
heart of tears and his masterpiece of lies is complete.

An empty page in an empty book,
An empty face casts an empty look

Her journal still lay beside him, still empty and still cold. She had
written him no warning. He had questions and held lies.

An empty ring on an empty wife,
An empty world chooses empty life

Vase

Beauty and harmony
Adorning a quiet table
Alleviating the mundane
Just because it's able

Ring

Two voices raised in harmony
Though neither one can sing
Their rejoicing is surrounding
The blessing of a ring

The promise that is made
Brings them both to tears
The joys that surround them
Suffice to calm all fears

A beautiful shining promise
Made between two souls
Life together binds them
They both are now made whole

Chapter Two
Politically Incorrect and Funny

I am tired of trying to please everyone. I am tired of walking on eggshells across that which might offend. Laughter is healthy. The sooner we learn to laugh with one another, the sooner we can take pleasure in our differences and enjoy the commonality of life.

Mr. Fiddle

I once knew a man who knew little
What he knew was to whittle and fiddle
The unruly children would mock and belittle
This poor little man and his fiddle
One day the rowdy boy Diddle
Turned up having turned to a fiddle
They asked the man who knew little
Just what happened to little boy Diddle
He said he was a man who knew little
But he knew how to whittle a fiddle of Diddle

The Moon

The moon will wax
And the moon will wane
But for all its effort
It's all in vain
For the moon will wax
And the moon will wane
And it will do this
Again, again, and a-gain

Dinosaurs

I haven't the faintest idea in mind
For why the dinosaurs were left behind
Perhaps they quarreled or made such a mess
That they simply could not, join with the rest
Or maybe they never existed at all
And the bones were planted by Angels in fall
It was all meant to be a cosmic joke
And now all the Angels, in laughter we soak

A Moment Inside the Mind of an Insecure Woman

(A woman walks into a store to buy milk)

"How could I have run out of milk?! I just want a glass of tea. Most people don't even need milk for tea. Do I have to do everything different? Oh, pears are on sale. I don't need pears…I need celery. I heard that celery helps you lose weight. Where did I hear that? I am incapable of remembering anything. Where did I hear that? It's probably not even true. I'm so gullible. What kind of milk should I get? Low fat. Real funny. I don't need low fat. No, but I certainly don't need more fat. (Catches reflection in glass). Wow, maybe I should work on my face before I work on my figure. If I don't fix my figure no one will ever look at anything but my face. Not like that's a bad thing, I have a great personality. Wow, how many times have I been blown off with that line? Matt, Dave, Zach, Chris…I don't even have a good personality. I am way too sensitive. I am high maintenance; I'm stupid…I'm insecure. Men hate women that are insecure, why would anyone ever like me? Hey, celery! That's a ridiculous price though. There are too many anorexics in the world; they are ruining the curve for the rest of us. (A young man walks by). Dang, not bad. What am I thinking? Am I seriously checking out a guy in the super market? Like he would give me the time of day. He didn't even see me. I would make a great spy. No one would ever notice me. I bet I could walk off the golden gate bridge at rush hour without anyone seeing me. Or maybe they just wouldn't care. I don't think I would want to jump off a bridge though. Pills are easier. Speaking of pills, vitamin C, I need to get some of that. Wow, how long have I been here? I mean, I know exactly where the milk is and yet

I walked all the way around the store. What was that? (Guy walks past again). And I'm still invisible. I think it is fantastic that I get to die alone. (A little girl walks past). Oh, I want one of those. I remember being one of those. What happened to me? I was five and I had dreams and ambitions. I knew prince charming would come for me. Yeah, that just shows that I have been stupid my whole life. (Grabs milk and walks to check out). That took forever. I don't like lines. There are rules for these sorts of things. I mean that lady is ten inches from me, but we can't speak. We just stand here. It's like I'm alone everywhere. An entire world of stupid bubble people."

"That will be $3.17," the cashier says.

"I forgot my wallet. I am officially the stupidest person ever."

Wandering

It is not the brightest thing I see
To let my mind go roaming free
Because apparently all it wants to be
Is far, so very far, away from me

Insecurity

I don't know what it is about me
But I certainly don't like what I see

Marriage

If you're not ready to be married
I would not recommend you do
Because the only one less comfortable
Will be the one married to you

Divorce

Divorce is more common than annulment
And paid out in monthly installments
Can save you the hassle of the wife at home
But may cost you interest and a thirty year loan

Weather

The weather is a safe conversation
When you know not the sexual orientation
It is proper to say the weather today
Is supposed to be…are you straight or gay?

Lemons

Lemons are the topic of choice
When you cannot decide by the voice
Whether it is proper to say he/she or she/he
And whether that he/she is looking at me/me

Politics

Politics are off limits to politicians
When speaking to primary physicians
For fear that their Republican asses
May end up exposed to the masses

Really

Darling boys will grow up to be men
But no woman quite remembers when

Those People

It is impolite to say 'those people'
Particularly gathered beneath a steeple
But once inside you're free to say
Liberal, lesbian, those people, and gay

Wrong Man

If you marry the wrong man
You are quite in a bind
For a loophole in the law
I am yet to find

Murder He Wrote

He wanted to kill his wife
That's what I heard the man say
He would have been locked up for life
If his wife hadn't killed him that day

Simply

Eloquence is simple
And simple quite complex
No one reads between the lines
If there's circles in the text

Off

When one says 'I'm off'
It is proper to explain
They are off to somewhere certain
Not certifiably insane

Monkey Butt

Monkey butt is the only nickname
My daughter has ever known
And one day when I'm older
She'll put me in a home

Charm

I'm having a charming evening
I've had a charming life
And I'll be rather charming
Until the day you call me wife

Government Agencies

"You need to see Mindy on the third floor," the receptionist said.

"Thank you," I replied and trudged up the stairs. What kind of sixty story building doesn't have an elevator? I mean, I understand the need for exercise and I am generally not a lazy person, but seriously!

"Hi, I'm hear to see Mindy about my situation that has already been explained to all the Right people and is only still a problem because the Right people were out of town and the Clueless people were sitting at their desks, so I had to climb the stairs to talk to Replacement people, and that is why I am here to see Mindy," I thought, while actually only saying, "I need to speak to Mindy, please, when you have time to let her know that I am here."

Forty-five minutes passed. Apparently, she didn't have time to let her know that I was here. The door had a label on it. It read, "This is the office of Someone Important, but currently you will find Mindy, the semi-important substitute sitting behind the desk." That was one of the longest door labels I had ever seen. Ten more minutes and I'm leaving, I thought. Twenty minutes passed. Finally the door open and Mindy called out, "Person with a problem who spoke to all the Clueless people while the Right people were away, please come in." I rose and walked toward the door. She looked at me and then pointed to a line ten feet from me. "No, no dear," she said. "You must wait in that line first."

There must have been twenty people already standing there, I waited for another hour. I finally came in and spoke to Mindy about my problem and the problem that I have had with fixing it due to the lack of Right people presently in the offices. She listened, or at least appeared to listen, for nearly twelve seconds before interrupting to point something out, "You see, my dear," she spoke with the same insincere ironic choice of words as before. "The Right people that were absent when you talked to the Clueless people were not in fact the Right people at all. They were the Right people for people whose problems have been resolved and simply need to go through processing. That obviously is not the case with you because I am aware that you still have a problem. You need to speak to the Right people in the planning department. They will know what to do with you darling."

"Where do I find the Right people from the planning department?" I asked.

"Thirty-third floor."

I walked to the stairwell and gazed longingly at the door three floors below me, but I went up.

I went to speak to the Right people, who turned out to be the Unauthorized Right people. They told me that they would be able to help me but that they did not have the authority to fix my problem. They directed me to the Tyrant on the first floor and suggested that I tell him that I had their approval if it was to be approved.

I spoke with the Tyrant who said that they did not have the authority to say that it had their approval and he directed me to the Disciplinarians on the sixteenth floor to relay everything about the Unauthorized Right people that I had just told him.

After speaking with the Disciplinarians, they told me that my problem could still be resolved quite easily if I return to the Tyrant and remind him that I had a problem.

The Tyrant seemed very offended that I could even think that he had somehow forgotten about the problem and sent me to the Very Important people on the sixtieth floor.

I arrived at the offices of Very and Important on the sixtieth floor just the Secretary was grabbing her bag to leave.

"Please," I said. "I need to speak to Very Important people."

"I'm sorry mam," she said. "They've been on vacation for about two weeks now. Should be back next Thursday if you can come back."

I was in awe at the ridiculous functioning of this entire establishment. I was angered and wanted to scream. My thoughts began to drift over the ways to destroy such a place. Blackmail I considered and then I began to think of much more hostile ways of dealing with the situation.

"Is there anything I can do?" The Secretary asked.

My thoughts trailed off and I sat looking at her in complete wonder. She should be running this place.

"Mam," she asked again. "Can I do anything?"

I explained the entire situation. I explained my entire situation, my problem and my problem with everyone in that building, and she listened.

"You need to go to advising to speak to the Advisor on the twenty-second floor," she said.

"Thank you for being so helpful," I responded, hoping that she couldn't hear the screaming voices in my head.

I trudged to the office of the Advisor. I waited for many minutes before the receptionist let me in to see him. He listened, though I had tuned myself, and finally responded with, "Yes, I see. You need to speak Mindy, she is our semi-important substitute. She will be able to help you."

I thanked him and walked down the stairs to the first floor. I pushed the door open and returned to the real world. People bustled around me and I pulled out my cell phone to call my therapist.

"Yes, four thirty tomorrow will work. Yes. Thank you. See you then."

The Government

The Government has its own way of doing things
You can only imagine the chaos this brings
For one will say one thing and one another
Until everyone you talk to you just want to smother

The Senate

I respect the individual
But often despise the whole
For the mass of them together
Seems to compromise the goal

Mountain Mentality

If you turn around in my driveway
I'm likely to cut your throat
And if you do it twice
Your survival is quite remote

Pet Peeves

The lack of grammar in our schools
Is really quite concerning
But no one knows the rules no more
And the students ain't discerning

Stereotypes

The drama team's dramatic
The speech team is emphatic
The jock's are all athletic
And the cooking class's pathetic

Mom

My mother is quite crazy
It's nothing personal
In fact to be quite honest
I think that was her goal

Smell

There was a boy I knew quite well
Rumors say that he was swell
Being around him was hard as hell
But mostly just because of the smell

Honestly

If you were to be honest
How many lies you've told
I'm not counting just today
But all lies new and old

Can I Have Him with My Coffee?

I entered through a swishing door to the place fate would have me be. In a line for some time I waited until the moment of decision came upon me. "White chocolate mocha please. Or maybe a machiato…or a latte." The irritation of those behind me could be felt through the back of my neck. The warmth of my confusion flushed my face. I should have studied, I meant to know what it was that I desired. I stuttered and tried to form something of substance with my words but came up at a loss. The woman behind the counter was growing angry with my every, "Um." Embarrassed by my own indecisiveness I mumbled, "Just the mocha, thank you," slipped her a five and backed away from the line with my change.

I felt as though all eyes were watching me, judging me as I took my seat on one of the plush chairs by a coffee table. Why they needed a coffee table I truly do not know, for in a coffee shop you would assume that any old table would become a coffee table. Why this thought chose to come to me at the same moment that he passed by I also do not know.

I'm sure that my mouth gaped open as I watched him walk to a chair only feet from mine. His muscles moved so gracefully, and his eyes, oh his eyes. They were deep as Homer and the color of rich chocolate. My heart was beating swiftly to the sound of the steaming machines. He glanced in my direction and for a moment his gaze caught my own. In a panic, I stood and rushed to pick up my drink that I might depart the thoughts that I found rushing in this place. I held it in my trembling hands and almost lost my breath as he proceeded to walk towards me.

Now within a foot of me he broke the ramblings of my mind with the smoothness of his lips, "It truly is not fair." He said so calm and so serene. "You now hold my weakness in your hands, but I am yet to know yours." As he spoke his eyes met my coffee cup.

My gaze followed his and to my astonishment it was no more a mocha that I held than the earth remained to be thought flat. That is entirely beside the point. We both smiled and as I handed him the drink our hands touched, sparks flew everywhere. This was mostly due to the coffee machine catching fire and exploding. He rushed me towards the door and into the garden across from the store. He looked at me and I at him. Yes, I had entered through a swishing door to the place that fate would have me be. And needless to say, we lived happily ever after.

Lunacy

I fancy myself a lunatic
This is not to be taken lightly
I simply know myself too well
To be crazy only slightly

Wife

The hum drums of a normal life
Is a healthy pace for a young wife
But the husband who keeps all hours of night
Is surely soon to be out of sight

Husband

A husband ought to be kind
Loving and never stalking
But you also must remember
This is a wife who's talking

Women

Women are God's gift to men
Truer now than it was back then
For every man there will be a when
Where he'll turn to blame women for sin

Men

Men as a whole can't help themselves
They are really quite lost without us
But be mindful not to tell them
Or you'll find yourself under a bus

Couples

Couples can be embarrassing
To each other and to the world
Sometimes being around them
Will make you want to hurl

Dating

Dating is such a waste of time
And it all ends the same way
You date and date and date
And then finally run away

Dinner

Dinner is my favorite meal
Especially when it's free
I guess now come to think of it
Dating has been good to me

Men and Women

I have recently found myself contemplating the differences between men and women. There are many subtleties that can be exposed upon deep reflection and observation, but there are also blatant contradictions between the two sexes.

Subtleties can be distinguished as those things that are entirely, or nearly so, internal. Those things which allow for brief differences in mannerism or expression but are otherwise invisible save to the human heart. Those things which I must acknowledge as being wholly blatant lay in the realm of visible differences or obvious observable results of internal differences.

One of the things that I have been pondering is a man and a woman's way of dealing with anger or confrontation. The events that got me thinking along these lines can briefly be explained by relating two separate observances.

One evening, a few weeks past, I entered my living room to find one of my roommates, Alyssa, sitting quietly. Her facial expressions suggested that I ought not to pry into the motives behind her solitude.

Upon closer inspection I noted that my other roommate, Denise, had also isolated herself and could be found in one of the back bedrooms on the second floor of our modest home. She too seemed to silently express a warning to anyone who might seek to question her.

I heeded the unspoken advice.

I myself, having no reason whatsoever to fret over, settled into a comfortable chair on the patio.

As I began to absorb the fleeting rays of the setting sun, I wondered briefly if I ought to think upon the dramatic episode that lay just inside the sliding glass door. I am not prone to drama and the thought returned to whence it came.

Jane Austen flooded my head with a world I only dared to dream about. A gentleman walked through a beautiful park with an air about him that suggested that love was on his mind…this moment was shattered by a slamming door as Denise departed from the premises.

No sooner had her car rounded the corner than Alyssa, her silence apparently as broken as my own, came to seek companionship where it could be found. "I'm perturbed," she said harshly. Of course, her being a product of Southern California linguistics, she was certain to have chosen different wording than my memory serves me with.

Her explanation was so scattered that I found myself relating to Edith Wharton when she wrote, "For heaven's sake girl, make a fresh start! It would take an omniscient deity to understand what it is you are saying!"

My response of course was an amiable nod of understanding though I began to wonder if perturbed was not even the word she had intended and that mad, in the sanitarium sense of the word, was much more accurate. She was outraged at a situation that involved Denise.

I began to wonder, honestly speaking, I was wondering to begin with, why she was thus speaking to me and not to the culprit of the injustices against her. She felt it was simply not prudent to argue such trifles and that the entire situation was wholly unimportant.

This struck me in manner which I had not expected, since obviously it had been important enough to warrant an unspoken separation between the two women. It had also bore her much grief and contemplation based upon the lines on her forehead and the circles under her eyes.

Later that night, I had the extreme misfortune of hearing nearly the same account from Denise with the same illogical conclusion: not prudent and unimportant.

This is the mind of women and this is the approach to conflict: distract one's self until the situation itself decides to vanish into a pile of unresolved bitterness and anger.

The tension remained until both women became so accustomed to the awkwardness that they went on with each day in a manner that suggested ignorance of their own senses.

This took weeks and weeks of silence and avoidance and finally was settled by a glass of tea and a conversation that had absolutely nothing to do with the instance in question.

During the course of this process I grew tired of the uncontrolled estrogen loose within my midst and chose to drive to my childhood home for a weekend.

Two friends from my youth were in the midst of a heated argument when I arrived. The dispute eventually came to blows and I left them to sort it out.

Only a few hours later, I returned to find them playing basketball in the driveway like usual. Both were laughing and joking. Ten minutes of blows had settled it.

And that my friends, is what I would define as a blatant difference between men and women.

Puzzles

Puzzles can be puzzling
And people can be troubling
But the puzzle must keep jumbling
And the people can't stop doubling

Baby

If the baby wakes in silence
There's hope still for the day
But when the baby wakes up screaming
You'd best to stay away

Mommy

A mommy is a special thing
The good ones are but few
If you had one of the good ones
I'm certain that you knew

The Pope

Being that I'm not Catholic
The papacy is Greek to me
That doesn't mean if I saw a priest
I wouldn't know to flee

Judaism

Being Jewish is an art form
It takes practice and takes work
And if I ever fail at anything
Being disowned is just a perk

Fire

Fire can be delightful
And also rather frightful
Depends on if it's in your home
Or burning everything you own

Rain

Rain is rather dreary
And sunshine rather nice
Still I'd rather have the rain
Than a lot of falling ice

Trees

I think that trees are useful
They seem to help us out
But if one falls in the forest
Does the guy beneath it shout?

Employment

Employment is a burden
We all will sometime bear
Bosses on the other hand
I'd rather leave them there

Time

Time will wait for no man
I've heard it said before
But when my mother hollers "dinner"
Time stops right at her door

Love

Love can be a blessed thing
Or an empty tune you're forced to sing

Chapter Three
What Little I Know of Life,
Love, and Everything Else

The love we find in innocence is the love that never fades. This is what we cling to. The memories of that first kiss, of the nights looking at the stars, those are the hopes we carry with us for the rest of our lives. There is always a glimmer in our eyes when we think of that first touch. We spend the rest of our lives convinced that those moments will remain forever; perfect and complete.

Restless

He is sleeping peacefully
While my eyes refuse to rest
My mind wonders across him
And settles on his chest
Pressing my lips against his skin
And wishing to join his dreams
So gentle are his manners
Or so his silence seems
Embracing those last minutes
Held tightly in his arms
Quietly clinging to him
And his most endearing charms
I cannot bear to leave him
But the darkness draws me here
And with my final breath I say,
"One day my love, rest there"
My eyes close in distant slumber
And the darkness takes my hand
My body resting solemnly
As my spirit leaves this land
As I'm drawn away I glance
Upon his peaceful face
Knowing he is what was best
About this life and place

Touch

A simple touch
Hand on my shoulder
Remove him and
The world is colder

Awaiting

Dreams are waiting just beyond
The grasp of one who longs for them
They circle gently and rest upon
The eyes of one who waits for him
Images float on crimson tides
The sun slips into its waves
They serenade the tired soul
Whose weary mind behaves
Resting peacefully to the sound
Of his heartbeat next to she
Safe from daring tempests
Held tight in arms of he
The dawn is held at bay by dreams
That summon him closer still
Knowing their lies and the void beside
But knowing he one day will

Unspoken

Dreams we've kept forgotten
Words we've left unsaid
All spoken in the silence
Hidden now beneath the bed
Lying in wait are whispers
Reminders of what we were
Cobwebs in the attic
Still, shattered and unsure
Rustling leaves to disturb
The autumns of this life
Touching skin but separate
Here lies husband and wife
Past moments held safely
In tired hands that shake
Empty glass distorts reflections
Until the soul does break

Once

I once looked up to you
Back when you were here
I once thought I didn't care
Back when you were near

Just That

Beautiful dress
Quaint church
Finally ending
A lifelong search

Wedded bliss
Morning kisses
Loving the feeling
Of being "Mrs."

Baby born
Love surrounds
Another child
Our joy abounds

Moments pass
Cold silence
Love and closeness
Have gone since

Long day
Hard life
Sick and tired
Of being "wife"

Children crying
Husband gone
Could one more thing
Really go wrong?

Tears fall
Time bomb
An Angel says
"I love you mom"

Smile comes
Tears dry
Hold him close
And give a sigh

Life changes
Kids grow
Still so tired
He'll never know

Love lacking
Husband gone
Just about to
Not go on

Life ends
Finally resting
All of this
Just for testing

Laughter

Laughter breaks into a thousand pieces
All life's pain suddenly ceases
Honest eyes reveal life's way
And the darkest night is turned to day

Moving On

Somber words in sober thought
All that's here, all that's not
The moment came, then was gone
And in between, we all moved on

Grandma Betty

Darling, my darling
Come here to me
Climb up on my lap
Come sit on my knee
I'll tell of you of worlds
You're yet to see
And show you the woman
You one day will be

Sorrow

Sorrow leave me til the morrow
Charge me not for time I borrow
For interest wrought will cause me sorrow
So sorrow leave me til the morrow

Remembering

Remembering then
Like remembering now
Missing the sea
Looking over the bow
Lost in the present
Lost in the past
Neither moment
Was intended to last

Before

You saw me before I knew me
I asked you what you saw
You said you saw forever
And the beauty of winter's thaw
You spoke with love unchanging
Always, was all you said
And me, in my foolishness
Walked away instead

The Draw of the Stage

I found myself standing on a moral stage; the spotlight shining in my eyes. There was something in the air that night. There was something that radiated beauty. The presence of such nearly made me gasp.

I stood on a stage, just like this one. I played piano, just over there.

The audience sat in those same seats, their eyes fixed upon my fingers. It was not my hands that they praised. The music springing from them, it was the music that captivated them. Their eyes beheld the source of their ears delight and they marveled.

After a masterful display of musical beauty, my movements ceased and the silence came. For a fraction of a second, there was peace. Then, as if on cue, the crowd erupted in applause and the blush of pride rose to my face.

There is something of elegance about such as stage as can only be described accurately as the silent breath by which life first begins.

I was standing upon a stage, as I am now, taking my first breath. Somewhere in the distance my fingers still grace the keys and their sound fills the quiet air. The audience fills seats in wait of hearing something worthy of remembrance. They cannot hear the piano, but the notes continue to play as my voice becomes the instrument.

The night rests in wait of a speech that I am scarcely prepared to give. A speech on life and glory, but I cannot find the words.

I am standing in the middle of life, I am walking in majestic space, and my heart is still sitting there playing. I can feel the cool keys as my fingers bring life into them. I can taste the salt on my lips as my energy drips from my pores. I can see life.

The music of life is poured out upon the stage and overflows into the crowd. Laughter and dancing emerge from its notes and I see myself float away on the air.

My eyes close and I see the world anew.

Life, life and glory…life is taking in an honest breath for the first time and then the final time. And glory, glory is inhaling life with each breath in between.

To Play

To play is to breathe
With the utmost of ease
And only those moments
Fully can please

The Course

Daylight breaks across the sky
The day begins anew
Its warmth is spread beyond the eye
And carries away the dew

The dreamy morning slips away
Into a sudden noon
The air moves swiftly across the way
Rushing somewhere soon

The afternoon is met by breath
Soft and quiet still
Everything settles for early death
As light loses its will

The evening hovers upon the shore
Awaiting its own end
The sun steals away once more
Its light to others lend

Darkness disperses those from hell
And takes its lifeless throne
Giving leave to those who fell
Claiming them his own

Dawn surrounds the king of gloom
Releasing streams of light
Crushing thoughts of impending doom
And ruling over night

Lonely

Standing alone is not lonely
Being apart from that which you love
That is real pain and agony
Of which there is none above

Missing Him

Quietly aching
Bleeding to death
Each moment coming closer
To that final breath

An Open Bar

A rose is placed upon the grave
A silent plea for peace
She walks away in silence
From a pain that will not cease
A single tear rolls down her cheek
She knows that more will follow
Holding back the agony
Trying not to wallow
For ever and for always
The way it was meant to be
Clinging to his memory
To slake the misery
They spent their lives together
No moment was apart
And as cliché as it may seem
He always held her heart

Waiting

The silence was deafening. It was not that I was incapable of hearing him breathe. I was not in any way physically unable to be distracted by the hum of the refrigerator or the occasional purr of an engine coming down the street. It was simply that it all registered as pure unadulterated silence at the point that it entered my brain. There was nothing more to it.

I could not hear him breathe because my brain could only process the vibrant silence of night. And so, I sat there, in silence, waiting.

There was nothing particular to wait for, I was just waiting.

Looking back, through fresh eyes, I could compare it to the eve before an anticipated day. As a child and into my early youth, I remember sitting very still to watch the clock change to 12:01 am on the morning of my birthday. I was captivated by the second hand, almost holding my breath, as to not alter its course. It seemed to me, at that time, that something momentous was about to happen.

There had to be some magic that occurred in the seconds that I was changed into something older and wiser than I had been.

The silent waiting reminded me of those seconds and the hours that followed reminded me of the sinking feeling that occurred when the magic never came.

True

Froot Loops were meant to be eaten by color
Spaghetti was meant to hold only butter
When you find someone who knows it's true
You'll know you found the one for you

Stutter

The words you speak have found an ear
The thoughts you think I want to hear
Where there is time for one more verse
Do not waste it to just rehearse
I do not care for practiced lines
I do not notice painted signs
So stutter, but please speak your mind
It is your flaws I want to find
Listening to the most beautiful sound
The voice I hear when you're around
I wait impatient for each word
Being certain that each is heard
Echoing thoughts wrap us here
Even your silence I'm finding dear

Lost

Out a window
On a beaten street
There stands a soul
With aching feet
She sees no sun shining
Looking to a falling sky
All alone in a crowded world
Lost enough to wonder why
Scared and hurting
Screaming without a sound
Hoping against hope
That some hope might be found

Heartache

Broken and rejected
Without a way to cope
Nothing can cure the anguish
Once left without hope

Scarred

Touching you is easy
Reaching you is hard
I never knew the truth
How badly you were scarred

Darkness

Darkness brings with it an element of absolute humility. The day sheds light upon all that is wonderful and glorious. Amidst its rays, one is able to grasp the sheer eloquence of human shape and movement. Within the light of day there is nothing more treasured or more despised than the truth. The truth reveals itself to the handsome and the ugly in the same looking glass. The daylight spreads its honest lies throughout its given time. It tells those with glowing skin that they are valued more. It whispers to the awkward girl that love is not for her. It possesses an element of vicious intent and benign quiet. It is in the light of day that those with beauty flaunt it and those without are seen for being empty. The barren tree is mocked by nature as the sun moves about the sky. But in those finals moments, before light fully disappears, that which is bare and empty stands in shocking contrast to the shapeless night. It revels in its moment of inexpressible beauty as those with glowing skin watch their spotlight fade. Then it happens. The darkness floods across all that is and was throughout the day. It casts itself upon the pale fingers of the aged and the twinkling eyes of youth. Within it, each is seen as equal. There can be nothing more beautiful than breath in the hands of night. Every flower appears in a black abyss along with every thorn.

Anticipating

I could not but hold my breath
To hear what you would say
You replied with few words, simply
You are the reason for my day

Beside Me

Gazing upon a starry sky
At stars we cannot see
Knowing it doesn't matter
For you are here with me
Walking through a quiet park
Swinging on lonely swings
Sure that life is wholly good
For we know all that it brings
Holding hands and kissing softly
Unaware of life outside
Our full attention going
To the one right by our side
Quietly slipping into the morning
Watching our midnight fade
Cherishing the company
And the memories we made